CLASH OF THE CRYPTIDS

BIGFOOT VS. YETI

by Alberto Rayo

CAPSTONE PRESS
a capstone imprint

Published by Capstone Press, an imprint of Capstone
1710 Roe Crest Drive, North Mankato, Minnesota 56003
capstonepub.com

Copyright © 2026 by Capstone. All rights reserved. No part of this
publication may be reproduced in whole or in part, or stored in
a retrieval system, or transmitted in any form or by any means,
electronic, mechanical, photocopying, recording, or otherwise,
without written permission of the publisher.

Library of Congress Cataloging-in-Publication Data is available on
the Library of Congress website.

ISBN: 9798875225444 (hardcover)
ISBN: 9798875225390 (paperback)
ISBN: 9798875225406 (ebook PDF)

Summary: Two big, strong, and hairy creatures face off in a fierce
fight. Bigfoot and Yeti are very similar cryptids, but only one will come
out on top.

Editorial Credits
Editor: Ericka Smith; Designer: Hilary Wacholz; Media Researcher:
Rebekah Hubstenberger; Production Specialist: Tori Abraham

Image Credits
Alamy: VICTOR HABBICK VISIONS/SCIENCE PHOTO LIBRARY, 29 (yeti);
Getty Images: Big_Ryan, 12, 13, iStock/choness, 29 (trophy), iStock/
Chris Wilson, 5 (background top), iStock/Vac1, 5 (top), 6, 7, 23, 25, 26,
27, Rich Legg, 9, THEPALMER, 19; Shutterstock: Daniel Eskridge, cover
(top), 20-21, Design_Lands, 30, guidopiano, 18, JM-MEDIA, 10-11, Oliver
Denker, cover (bottom), Vac1, 15, Warpaint, 5 (bottom), 16-17, 24

Design Elements
Shutterstock: Ballerion, katsuba_art

Any additional websites and resources referenced in this book are not
maintained, authorized, or sponsored by Capstone. All product and
company names are trademarks™ or registered® trademarks of their
respective holders

Printed and bound in China.   006276

TABLE OF CONTENTS

LET'S RUMBLE! 4

A LITTLE HISTORY 8

A LOT ALIKE 12

A BIG BATTLE 22

Glossary 30

Read More 31

Internet Sites 31

Index 32

About the Author 32

Words in **bold** are in the glossary.

LET'S RUMBLE!

It's late. A loud stomp shakes the snow off tall trees. Two creatures quickly spot each other across a field. They're both huge, after all.

One grunts. He looks angry. He **darts** across the field. The other disappears into the snowy woods. But he won't stay hidden for long. There's about to be a BIG battle—between Bigfoot and Yeti.

Name: Bigfoot

Alias: Sasquatch

Type of Cryptid: Humanoid/Apelike

Height: 6 to 9 feet (1.8 to 2.7 meters) tall

Features: Tall, hairy, great strength

First Sighting: 1800s

Range (Area): Pacific Northwest, North America

Likes: Daily, 24-hour "me" time

Dislikes: Humans, photographs

Name: Yeti

Aliases: Meh-teh, Bun Manchi, the Abominable Snowman

Type of Cryptid: Humanoid/Apelike

Height: 6 to 10 feet (1.8 to 3 m) tall

Features: Tall, hairy, great strength, long arms

First Sighting: 1832 (first sighting recorded in English)

Range (Area): The Himalayas, Nepal and Tibet

Likes: Long walks in the snow

Dislikes: Humans in his personal space

A LITTLE HISTORY

BIGFOOT'S BEEN AROUND

Bigfoot is from North America's Pacific Northwest. Native American people from the Spokane Tribe have long been telling stories about a creature that looks like Bigfoot! He's described as a tall, hairy creature.

Some people believe Bigfoot is related to a huge **prehistoric** ape that lived in Asia.

YETI OR NOT, HERE I COME!

Yeti lives in the snowy landscape of the Himalayas. Tibetan tales about him date back to the 1100s!

Some people think Yeti's just a brown bear. Brown bears can stand on two legs.

FACT
Yeti's most famous nickname is the "Abominable Snowman." Abominable? It's just a big word for "people hate him."

A LOT ALIKE

Physically, Bigfoot and Yeti share many traits! They're both hairy. They're both very tall and walk on two feet. And they have incredible strength, given their size.

Bigfoot and Yeti aren't just big and strong—they're clever too! Some people claim to have recordings of Bigfoot. In them, he communicates by grunting and whistling. And Yeti might be able to use tools.

MORE THAN JUST TWO BIG FEET!

Bigfoot is most famous for his feet. They leave BIG prints behind. He's reportedly between 6 and 9 feet (1.8 and 2.7 meters) tall. His fur is dark. He has a BIG brow ridge. And he stinks!

Many believe Bigfoot is an **omnivore**. That means he eats plants and animals.

FACT

One reported Bigfoot footprint found in the 1960s was about 18 inches (45.7 centimeters) long and 9.2 inches (23.4 cm) wide.

WHAT A REACH!

Yeti's main feature is his long arms. He also has a humanlike face. His fur has been described as brown, gray, or white. He's an omnivore too.

FACT
Yeti also has big feet! Why isn't he called Bigfoot?!

HARD TO FIND

Both Yeti and Bigfoot prefer **solitude**. And they are active mostly at night. But that doesn't stop **cryptid** scientists from trying to find them. And some people just have the bad—or good— luck of coming across Bigfoot or Yeti.

Many humans explore the forests of North America where Bigfoot lives. Sightings happen most often during the spring and summer. Bigfoot can get pretty angry when he encounters people.

Yeti's better at avoiding humans. Fewer people explore Yeti's home high in the Himalayas. But he can be kind—or terrifying—when he is spotted.

A BIG BATTLE

Back to this snowy battle. Since Yeti is excellent at hiding, this battle could be decided by which beast attacks the other first. Can Bigfoot find Yeti before he can attack from his hiding place?

Bigfoot moves swiftly through the trees, looking for Yeti. Bigfoot spots Yeti and attacks. Yeti almost gets hit! But he blocks the blow with a long arm.

Yeti tries to hit Bigfoot, but he's not quick enough. Bigfoot lands a punch! They exchange powerful blows, but Yeti knows that he can only take so many.

Yeti goes on the defensive, blocking Bigfoot's blows with his long arms again.

Bigfoot's fierce punches eventually break through! Bigfoot lands a **vicious** blow—right to Yeti's face! Yeti falls to the ground.

But Bigfoot's tired now. That last punch took everything out of him. He just hopes Yeti doesn't get up.

But Yeti does get up. He's not tired yet. He takes a few steps back, to put distance between them. He launches a swift punch with his long arm that lands on Bigfoot's chin. Bigfoot falls down! And he doesn't get up.

NOT BUYING IT? Who do you think comes out on top when Bigfoot and Yeti CLASH?

GLOSSARY

cryptid (KRIP-tihd)—creatures whose existence has not been proven

dart (DART)—to move quickly

omnivore (OM-nuh-vohr)—an animal that eats both plants and animals

prehistoric (pree-hi-STOR-ik)—living or occurring before people began to record history

solitude (SOL-ih-tood)—being alone

vicious (VISH-uhss)—fierce or dangerous

READ MORE

Hubbard, Ben. *What Do We Know About the Yeti?* New York: Penguin Workshop, 2024.

Peterson, Megan Cooley. *The Secret Life of Bigfoot*. North Mankato, MN: Capstone, 2023.

Williams, Dinah. *Bigfoot*. Jefferson City, MO: Scholastic, 2025.

INTERNET SITES

Britannica Kids: Abominable Snowman
kids.britannica.com/kids/article/Abominable-Snowman/390061

Britannica Kids: Bigfoot
kids.britannica.com/students/article/Bigfoot/631810

Kiddle: Cryptozoology Facts for Kids
kids.kiddle.co/Cryptozoology

INDEX

Bigfoot,
   communication, 4, 13
   feet, 14–15
   first sighting, 6
   food, 14
   nicknames, 6, 9
   range, 6
   size, 6
   smell, 14
brown bears, 10

Himalayas, 7, 10, 20
humans, 6, 7, 8, 10, 13, 18, 19, 20

Pacific Northwest, 6, 8

scientists, 18
Spokane Tribe, 8

Tibet, 7, 10

Yeti,
   arms, 16, 22, 25, 28
   feet, 16
   first sighting, 7
   food, 16
   nicknames, 7, 10
   range, 7
   tools, 13

ABOUT THE AUTHOR

Alberto Rayo is a writer from Lima, Perú. He loves science fiction that feels like fantasy, fantasy that feels like science fiction, and monsters (because they're cooler than humans). When he's not writing comics, he's writing prose. And when he's not writing prose, he might be sleeping.